GW00597226

THE HUMOUR OF CORK

THE HUMOUR OF CORK

DES MACHALE

MERCIER PRESS

MERCIER PRESS
PO Box 5, 5 French Church Street, Cork
16 Hume Street, Dublin 2

© Des MacHale 1995

ISBN 1 85635 125 4

A CIP for this book is available from the British Library.

10 9 8 7 6 5 4 3 2 1

This book is sold subject to the condition that it shall not, by way of
trade or otherwise, be lent, resold, hired out or otherwise circulated
without the publisher's prior consent in any form of binding or cover
other than that in which it is published and without a similar condition being imposed on the subsequent purchaser.

Printed in Ireland by Colour Books Ltd.

DEDICATION

It is with very great reluctance, and under the threat of legal proceedings, that I dedicate this book to my friend and protagonist Professor John A. Murphy, who fondly believes that all the stories in this book are his.

INTRODUCTION

I am not a Corkman (Heaven forbid) but I have lived for nearly twenty-five years in this dear old city by the Lee, long enough to have absorbed some of the peculiar sense of humour of the place. Cork is unique in that it has its own distinctive brand of humour – as indicative of the place as is the River Lee, the Bells of Shandon or Cork hurling. Most humour nowadays is international and with modern technology the quip that originates in New York is told within a few minutes in London, Tokyo and Melbourne, with approximately the same level of understanding and appreciation. Not so the humour of Cork – it takes years, maybe even a lifetime, to appreciate and understand its subtlety. Like good whiskey, it has to mellow and be savoured, and I freely admit that after all these years I am only just beginning to come to grips with it.

Above all, the Corkman feels that he is superior (and why wouldn't I, boy?) not just to his fellow countrymen and his fellow Europeans, but to all mankind. He is always way ahead of you, boy. In this there is no malice, no arrogance, no falsehood, just an acceptance of the way things are. You have to fight to have your talent recognised in Cork, but when you make it, Cork people are always generous in their praise. Watch, however, for the sting in the tail, the moment when you relax basking in the glory of Cork praise, because this is the very moment the boot goes in. In fact, this is the very essence of Cork humour.

I have collected the stories in this book over many years and the vast majority of them are endemic to the Cork region and are not to be found elsewhere. I would like to thank my very many friends in Cork from whom I have heard many of these stories either by word of mouth or from their writings, stage, radio, and television shows. In particular, I acknowledge my debt to John A. Murphy, Niall Tóibín, Matt Murphy, Dick Haslam, Michael Twomey, Frank Duggan, Billa O'Connell, Paddy Comerford, George Sullivan, Michael O'Connell, Din Joe Fitzgibbon, and those two late great jokers Captain Seán Feehan and James N. Healy.

Cork's humour is Ireland's humour at its best and finest, despite what Dublin, Galway and Belfast will say. I have chosen to present the humour of Cork in the form of stories and anecdotes centred on real or imaginary characters. I hope that this book will be only the beginning of its understanding and appreciation by a national and international audience. If you are new to Cork, you are in for a treat, and even if you're not new to Cork, there are still a few laughs in store for you because nobody knows, or could know, all the humour of Cork. Enjoy!

A rather prim and proper Cork lady had a number of prize cats and one of them was a little under the weather. So she called the vet and after a quick examination the vet said, 'There is nothing wrong with your cat – it's the most natural thing in the world. She's going to have kittens.'

'But that is impossible,' said the lady, 'she hasn't been out of my sight since the moment she was born, and she has never been near a tomcat.'

'What about him over there?' said the vet, pointing to a tomcat sitting on a couch smiling to himself.

'Don't be ridiculous,' said the lady, 'that's her brother.'

***

Have you heard about the Corkman who went to America and made big money? Unfortunately he's in jail, because he made the money a quarter of an inch too big.

***

A Japanese businessman on a visit to Cork told his host that he was delighted to hear fluent Japanese being spoken in Cork. As he crossed Patrick's Bridge he heard two Corkmen talking to each other and their conversation went something like 'O'Hora, O'Hara, oo hoor oo, how are oo?'

Cornelius was driving home to a Cork suburb one evening and on his way hit several trees, a telegraph pole and knocked down several pedestrians. Eventually he was stopped by a guard who breathalysed him and said, 'Do you realise sir that you are three times over the legal limit?'

'Thank God for that,' said Cornelius, 'I thought the steering was gone in the ould Merc!'

***

What do you call a lamp post in Cork?
A leisure centre.

***

Why did God create alcohol?
To prevent Corkmen from taking over the world.

***

A professional medical man in Cork once decided to further his career by taking an MD degree at the university. He chose to specialise in gynaecology and took as his research topic the female reproductive cycle. He was known afterwards for many years as 'the menstrual boy'.

An old Corkman carrying a bottle of whiskey and in a well-oiled condition, was met by his Parish Priest as he staggered down the street (the Corkman, not the Parish Priest).

'Con, Con,' said the Parish Priest, 'what will you say to Saint Peter when you arrive at the Golden Gates?'

Con looked at him and said, 'I'll say "cock-a doodle do".'

***

Why do Cork traffic wardens have yellow lines on their caps?

So people won't park their cars on their heads.

***

Cork's Coal Quay is one of the most colourful markets in the country and must be one of the few places where pounds, shillings and pence are still the favoured currency. One old lady there in charge of her stall said that the new fangled decimal currency would never catch on in the Coal Quay and that it was particularly unfair on all the old people who had been used to the other system all their lives. With flawless logic she asked, 'Why didn't they wait until all the old people were dead before introducing it?'

There is an old saying in Cork that you should never ask a man where he comes from. The reasoning behind it goes like this: if he is from Cork, he will tell you soon enough, but if he is not, why embarrass him?

***

Once upon a time there were two Corkmen – now look how many there are.

***

A very successful Cork businessman was boasting over brandy and cigars at his club, about how poor his family had been when he was a child. 'For the first three years,' he told his listeners, 'I never went out because I didn't have a stitch of clothes to wear. Then, when I was four, my father bought me a cap and I used to sit looking out the window.'

***

A rich Corkman was being pestered by his son to buy him a Mickey Mouse outfit for Christmas, so he bought him the Limerick hurling team.

***

An English businessman was staying at a little hotel in West Cork and left strict orders for a call at eight o'clock the next morning.

He was woken next morning by the porter knocking loudly on his door shouting out, 'Was it six o'clock or seven o'clock you wanted to be called at, sir?'

'Eight o'clock,' said the Englishman irritably, 'what time is it now?'

'Ten o'clock,' said the porter.

***

A Corkwoman was very proud of her daughter's academic prowess. When an important man called to her house, she introduced her daughter to him as follows: 'This is my daughter Mary who took first place in Ireland in both French and Algebra. Mary, say something to the gentleman in Algebra.'

***

Two Corkwomen were talking at the bus stop.

'I don't know what to get my son for Christmas,' said one to the other.

'Why don't you get him a book?' suggested the second.

'Don't be daft, girl,' was the reply, 'he have a book already.'

A Cork travel agent looked out through his window to see an old lady and an old man gazing longingly at his display of posters for exotic holiday resorts. As a publicity gimmick, he decided to offer them a free round-the-world cruise with all expenses paid.

When they returned home some months later, he asked the old lady if she had enjoyed herself.

'Wonderfully,' she replied, 'but tell me one thing, who was that old man that I had to sleep with every night?'

***

Some years ago there was a competition to find a motto for Cork's famous Blarney Castle. The winning entry was: *Póg mo stone*

***

A Dubliner went to live in Cork but unfortunately he died. Two Corkmen went around from house to house collecting money to give him a decent burial.

'Excuse me, sir,' they said to one old Corkman, 'would you contribute £1 to bury a Dubliner?'

'Look,' said the ould fellow, 'here's £10 – bury ten of them.'

***

Con and Jeremiah were playing golf together at Muskerry Golf Club. Con is lining up a crucial putt when he looks up and sees a funeral procession going by. He stops, stands to attention, takes off his golf cap and holds it over his heart until the funeral has passed by.

'Now that's what I call a real Christian gesture,' said Jeremiah, 'and at such a vital stage in the match too.'

'It was the least I could do,' said Con returning to his putt, 'after twenty-five years of marriage to her.'

***

What is the difference between a Cork lawyer and a Cork doctor?

A Cork lawyer merely robs you; a Cork doctor robs you and kills you as well.

***

Con was asked to take his sister's twin babies, a boy and a girl, to the church to be christened.

'What names do you want them called?' he asked her.

'I'd like the girl to be called Denise,' said his sister, 'and you choose a name for the boy yourself.'

After the ceremony, Con arrived home and presented the twins to her.

'Here they are,' he told her, 'and they are called Denise and Denephew.'

DE PAPER

It is said that the definition of a well-read Corkman is a fellow who reads both the *Examiner and* the *Echo*. The *Cork Examiner* and the *Evening Echo* are two of Ireland's best loved newspapers, and I find it impossible to believe that some of the items I have collected from their columns over the years were not meant to be funny – jokes perpetrated by columnists and editors with a twinkle in their eye to liven up the sad and serious news.

For example, when the *Titanic* sank, the *Examiner* ran the headline:

West Corkman Lost at Sea.

More recently, a woman from Kerry gave birth to triplets in a Cork hospital. On the same day, three IRA men involved in a kidnapping were surrounded in a wood in County Leitrim. One was captured but the other two escaped. The *Examiner* ran the following two headlines side by side:

Kerrywoman gives Birth to Triplets

Gardai Still Looking for Other Two Men.

Other memorable *Examiner* headlines include:

Pope Dies for Second Time in a Month

Man Stated to be Critical Following Fatal Accident

Body of Man Found in Graveyard

Priceless Tipperary Chalice Worth £5.5M

Murphy Trophy Cup Presented for Cow with Best Udders in Memory of Mrs Mary Murphy

The *Evening Echo* too is no slouch when it comes to conscious and unconscious humour. Strangely enough, the obituary columns of the *Echo* have given many a chuckle to Corkonians over the years. Here are a few examples:

The death has occurred in Cork of Mr Alfred L. O'Sullivan, the well-known secret agent.

Underneath an *In Memoriam* notice for her late husband, instead of a verse from the bible, a Corkwoman had inserted 'You'd be alive today if you did what I told you.'

Now there is a new concept for you, post-mortem nagging!

17

There was a lovely account of the burial of a much-loved ninety-five year old woman from Macroom which the *Evening Echo* reported as follows: During the course of the burial, the son-in-law of the deceased collapsed by the graveside and had to be rushed to hospital. This naturally cast a gloom over the entire proceedings.

Another sad story concerned an unfortunate man found dead in his flat on Christmas day. The inquest reported that 'on Christmas Eve, the dead man made his way along Barrack Street.'

Right enough, you do meet a lot of fellows looking like that in Cork around Christmas time!

Cork newspapers are famous too for their small ads. Here are a few classics:

Passport for sale. Never used. Owner leaving the country.

For sale, a quantity of port drunk by Queen Victoria on her visit to Cork.

Lost, Blackpool area, bald one-eyed ginger tomcat, crippled in both legs, recently castrated, answers to name of 'Lucky'.

Young farmer wishes to meet eligible girl with tractor. Please enclose photograph (of tractor).

For sale: New Mercedes in perfect working order – £100 or nearest offer. As advertised on TV's *Crimewatch*.

Retraction: Instead of being jailed for murdering his wife by pushing her downstairs and throwing a lighted oil lamp after her as we reported last week, we believe that the Reverend Roger McIntosh in fact died unmarried four years ago.

When the *Examiner* once announced that it was increasing its price by five pence on the following Monday, an enterprising Corkman went out and bought up all the copies he could find on Saturday.

A Frenchman visiting Cork was under the impression that the *Cork Examiner* was a specialist in the wine trade.

It was the biggest funeral that Cork had ever seen. There were thousands upon thousands of men marching behind the hearse and at their head was a man leading a muzzled alsatian dog. A passer-by was intrigued at all this so he asked the man what was going on.

'It's my wife's funeral,' said the man, 'and she was savaged to death by the dog.'

'I see,' said the passer-by, 'would it be possible to borrow that dog?'

'Get to the end of the queue,' said the man.

***

There was always a healthy rivalry between the Catholic and Protestant bishops of Cork. In the nineteenth century, when the Protestant bishop of Cork died, the Catholic bishop is reputed to have remarked, 'Now at last he knows who the real Bishop of Cork is.'

***

Con was applying to join his local hurling team.

'What experience do you have?' the captain asked him.

'Well I once played with Christy Ring,' said Con.

'Can you prove that?' asked the captain.

'Well,' said Con, 'after a game one of the fellows said to me, "If you're a hurler, I'm Christy Ring".'

What do you call a Cork parachutist?

Condescending.

***

Have you heard about the nine year old Cork boy who played chess blindfold simultaneously against twelve International Grandmasters?

He was annihilated in all twelve matches.

***

Con's favourite game was hurling – no other game had any thrills, excitement or skill – it was hurling, hurling, and only hurling.

One afternoon he was watching hurling with his friends on television when a golf match appeared on the screen. As he turned away in disgust, his friends asked him to have a look at it for a few minutes. And what a golf tournament it was! Jack Nicklaus was on the last green needing to sink a sixty foot putt to win the Open. Nicklaus lined up the putt and rammed it into the hole from sixty feet to win the tournament to a deafening round of applause and loud cheering.

'Well,' said Con's friends, 'now will you admit that Nicklaus showed great skill in sinking that putt?'

'Sure why wouldn't he?' said Con, 'there wasn't a man within ten yards of him.'

There is a village in West Cork reputed to be the healthiest village in Ireland. They had to shoot a fellow to start a cemetery. Only one person has died there over the last twenty years. He was the local undertaker and he died of starvation.

***

An old Corkman died and by tradition there was a wake for three days (to make sure he was really dead and not just dead drunk!) His widow imbibed rather heavily of portwine and became a little confused. As midnight, the traditional time for the saying of the rosary for the eternal repose of the soul of the deceased approached, she knew there was something she had to do, but couldn't remember quite what it was. Finally, she called for silence and said 'We'll have three cheers for the holy souls in Purgatory.'

***

Have you heard about the Corkman who was considered to be cleverer that Einstein?

Well, it is said that only four people could understand Einstein's Theory of Relativity, but the Corkman's theory – nobody could understand it!

***

An American tourist arrived at the tourist office in Cork and in a confused state asked, 'On which side of the river is Patrick's Bridge?'

***

Why do Corkmen take such an instant dislike to Dubliners?
It saves time.

***

It has been said that Cork has the best climate in the world, but the weather ruins it.

***

Cork golf clubs and tennis clubs are often quite uncrowded during summer months. Sure if you were playing golf or tennis, everyone would know you didn't have a yacht!

***

A month after he got married, Con began to wonder if he had made the right decision. Every meal his new wife cooked for him consisted of wedding cake and chips.

Con and his friend Jeremiah were talking in the pub one afternoon when Con mentioned that he was planning to paint his garden fence green but hadn't a drop of green paint in the house. Jeremiah told him that he had a big pot of green paint and to call over for it.

So that evening, Con knocked at his friend's door only to be met by his wife in tears.

'Is Jeremiah at home?' he enquired.

'No,' sobbed the wife, 'he died about an hour ago.'

'Before he passed away,' said Con, 'did he say anything about a pot of green paint?'

***

At a party in Dublin, a wind-broken soprano who had seen better days was asked to sing. She launched into 'The Banks of my own Lovely Lee' and as she finished she noticed a little grey-haired old man sitting quietly in the corner sobbing into his drink. So she took his hand and said to him 'Are you a Corkman, sir?'

'No, madam,' he replied, 'I am a musician.'

***

Why are there so many great Cork pianists and so few great Cork violinists?

Have you ever tried balancing a pint of stout on a violin?

A Corkwoman was visiting Dublin Zoo for the first time. One of the cages she stopped at was that of the kangaroo. Over the cage was a notice:

A native of Australia.

'Holy mother of God,' she shrieked, 'to think that me sister is married to one of dem tings.'

***

A Corkman and his wife were having marriage difficulties so they decided to visit a marriage counsellor. It took her a long time to get to the root of their problems but eventually she decided that the Corkman was not arousing his wife sufficiently before lovemaking and was not familiar enough with the female anatomy.

'For example,' she asked him, 'do you know where the clitoris is?'

'Is it near Mullingar?' said the Corkman.

***

The definition of a true Corkman is someone who would go into a revolving door behind you and come out in front of you.

***

In the days of the old Soviet Union, a Cork businessman was visiting Moscow and his hosts assumed that he wanted to pay his respects at the tomb of Lenin. Now he had no inclination whatsoever to do this, but to please them he pretended that he was very keen. It seems that nobody, but nobody, jumps the long queue at the tomb of Lenin, so he stood for nearly three hours in temperatures of about minus thirty, shuffling along, until he finally reached the tomb which was surrounded by four Russian guards standing stiffly to attention. As he passed by the last of them he whispered in his ear, 'Didn't he go very sudden in the end?'

***

A Corkman was going through some of his grandfather's old belongings in the attic when he came across a ticket for a pair of shoes being repaired back in the 1940s. The firm was still in business, so he took the ticket down to the shop and showed it to the lady at the counter who took it into the back of the shop. She emerged a few minutes later and said, 'They will be ready on Thursday.'

***

A Corkman had an inferiority complex. But he claimed it was the biggest and most complicated inferiority complex in the world.

Con's next-door neighbour had died and was lying in his coffin with a great big smile on his face.

'Why is he smiling?' Con asked the man's widow.

'Well, it's like this,' she told him. 'He died in his sleep and he doesn't know he's dead yet. He's dreaming he's still alive and what I'm afraid of is that if he wakes up and realises he's dead, the shock might kill him.'

***

Alexander Bell, who invented the first telephone, was a pretty bright fellow, but the real genius was the Corkman who invented the second telephone. But when Bell rang him up the line was engaged.

***

'Gentlemen of the jury,' shouted the crier in a Cork court, 'please proceed to your accustomed places.'

The court erupted as the twelve jurymen proceeded to cram themselves into the dock.

'Silence in court,' shouted the judge above the noisy din, 'or I'll have all you blackguards who aren't lawyers cleared from the court.'

***

Did you know that if a Corkman moves to Dublin he increases the level of intelligence in both counties?

***

A Cork lady was having a passionate affair with an inspector from the corporation. One afternoon they were carrying on in the bedroom together when her husband arrived home unexpectedly.

'Quick,' said the lady to her lover, 'into the wardrobe,' and she bundled him in stark naked.

The husband however became suspicious and after a search of the bedroom discovered your man in the wardrobe.

'Who are you?' he asked him.

'I'm an inspector from the corporation.'

'What are you doing in there?'

'I'm investigating a complaint about an infestation of moths.'

'And where are your clothes?'

The man looked down at himself and said, 'The little bastards.'

***

Con was the most superstitious Corkman in the world. He wouldn't work on any week with a Friday in it.

First Corkman: I see where Paddy Murphy has just run a hundred metres in six seconds.

Second Corkman: That's impossible, the world record is over nine seconds.

First Corkman: Paddy Murphy found a shortcut.

***

The great Henry Ford, the motor magnate, once visited Cork and offered £5,000 to a local hospital. A local newspaper, however, ran the headline:

Ford offers £50,000 to Cork Hospital

knowing that such a rich man would not quibble over an extra zero. Ford saw the game very well and asked if he could have a verse from the Bible on the memorial beside his name.

'Certainly,' he was told, 'what verse would you like?'

'I was a stranger, and you took me in,' smiled Ford.

***

A Corkman received a bill for £30 from his shoemaker, so he sent the following reply.

'I never ordered those shoes, and if I did you never sent them, and if you did I never got them, and if I did I paid for them, and if I didn't, I won't.'

'Did you hear about Jimmy McCarthy?' said one Cork-woman to another.

'No, what happened to him?' said the second.

'A big steam hammer dropped a hundred feet onto his chest and killed him.'

'I'm not a bit surprised,' said the second Cork-woman, 'all the McCarthys had weak chests.'

***

An old West Corkman and his wife were on a visit to Dublin. They decided to have a meal in an expensive restaurant where they ordered a four-course dinner with steak as the main course. When the meal was served, the West Corkman tucked in while his wife sat looking at him for over twenty minutes.

'What is the matter, madam,' asked the head waiter, 'isn't the meal to your satisfaction?'

'Certainly it is,' said the old lady with relish, 'but I'm waiting for Pa to be finished with the teeth.'

***

Why won't a shark attack a Cork lawyer?
Professional courtesy.

***

Con and Jeremiah were talking in a pub.

'I wouldn't go to America if you paid me,' said Con.

'Why is that?' said Jeremiah.

'Well for one thing they all drive on the right hand side of the road there.'

'And what's wrong with that?' said Jeremiah.

'Well,' said Con, 'I tried it driving to Dublin the other day, and it's terrible.'

***

A funeral was making its way up Patrick's Hill in Cork city. The back door of the hearse had not been properly secured however, so on the huge slope the coffin slid out and began to travel all the way down the hill. So great was its momentum that it travelled across Patrick's Bridge, down Patrick Street into a chemist's shop where it came to rest with a bang against the counter. The lid flew off and the corpse rose slowly saying to the startled assistant, 'Can you give me something to stop me coffin?'

***

A Cork doctor was treating a patient for jaundice for ten years until he found out the fellow was Chinese.

Worse still, he cured him!

31

A Cork businessman saved up all his life for a trip to Rome. He saw all the wonderful artistic sights of the Eternal City and the highlight of the trip was when he went on a guided tour of the Sistine Chapel. As he and the party gazed upward at the ceiling of the Chapel, Michelangelo's masterpiece, he was asked what he thought of it.

'Yerra, 'tis all right I suppose,' said the Corkman, 'but you should see the ceiling of the Provincial Bank in Cork.'

***

When Bernadette's father died she went to the undertaker's to buy a traditional Cork shroud.

'How much are they?' she asked the undertaker.

'Twenty pounds,' he told her.

'Twenty pounds!' she said in disgust, 'I can get one for ten pounds down town.'

'Those are of inferior quality ma'am,' he told her, 'the corpse would have his knees out through it in a week.'

***

'Politicians,' said Con, 'like babies' nappies, should be changed often, and for the same reason.'

$\mathbf{A}$ West Cork man was in the arrival lounge of Cork Airport when he got into conversation with an American lady.

'I'm waiting to meet my brother,' he told her. 'He's been in America for forty years, and we haven't clapped eyes on each other in all that time.'

'How exciting,' she said to him, 'I wonder if you will recognise him when he gets off the plane?'

'Not a chance,' he replied, 'I haven't seen even a photograph of him in all that time.'

'And I wonder,' she continued, 'if he will recognise you?'

'Sure why wouldn't he?' he said to her. 'I haven't been away at all.'

***

$\mathbf{'I}$'ll have to charge you,' said the guard to a West Corkman driving his donkey cart into the city, 'because your name is obliterated.'

'Indeed it is not obliterated,' was the reply, ''tis O'Sullivan.'

A Corkwoman finally persuaded her husband to take her to an operatic concert after many years of trying. Afterwards, she said to him, 'Didn't the soprano have a lovely repertoire?'

'Yes,' he agreed, 'and that dress she was wearing showed it off to the best advantage.'

***

Con went on *Mastermind* and chose as his special subject the Irish Rebellion of 1916.

'Who was the leader of the rebellion?' asked Magnus Magnusson.

'Pass,' said Con.

'Where did the rebellion take place?'

'Pass,' said Con.

'How many people signed the declaration of independence?'

'Pass,' said Con.

'Good man, Con,' came a voice from the audience, 'tell them nothing.'

A Corkman won a million and a half pounds in the National Lottery so he rushed round to his parents' house to tell them the good news.

'I've just won a million and a half in the National Lottery,' he told them, 'and the first thing I'm going to do is to give each of you a hundred pounds, to be spent on whatever you want.'

'Look son,' said his father, 'there is something I've been meaning to tell you. Money was scarce when your mother and I were courting, so the truth of the matter is, we never actually got round to getting married.'

'Oh my God,' said the Corkman, 'you know what that makes me?'

'Yes,' said his father, 'and a mean one at that.'

***

A Corkwoman prayed to God every night that she might win the National Lottery but there was no sign of any prize coming her way. So she prayed even harder and still there was no sign of a prize. Finally, in exasperation, she went into the church and shouted out, 'God, what do I have to do to win the lottery?'

And the voice of God boomed back, 'Well you could buy a ticket for a start.'

***

A baby camel was asking his mother some questions about life.

'Why do we have humps mammy?' he asked her.

'So we can go up to eight days without water,' she told him.

'And why do we have long eyelashes?'

'So the desert sandstorms won't blow sand into our eyes.'

'And why do we have such big wide feet?'

'So we won't sink in the sand.'

'Just one more question mammy.'

'What's that son?'

'What the hell are we doing here in Fota Zoo?'

***

Con was at his barber having his monthly cut-price haircut.

'Have you been anywhere since I saw you last?' asked the barber.

'I've been on holiday,' said Con, 'in Italy.'

'And what did you do there?'

'I had a personal audience with the Pope,' said Con.

'And what did you say to him?'

'It's a great pleasure to meet your holiness,' said Con.

'And what did he say to you?'

'He said, "who gave you the bloody awful haircut?"'

CORK SIGNS AND NOTICES

There is a great tradition in Cork of funny signs and notices. Most of them are written, one suspects, tongue-in-cheek, to attract attention. Here are some of the best of them that I have collected over the years.

Haircuts while you wait – one per customer only

In a pub: Just because your optician told you that you need glasses please don't take ours

Credit cheerfully given to all customers over the age of eighty – provided they are accompanied by their grandparents

Good clean entertainment in this pub every night except Tuesday

This street is a one way cul-de-sac at both ends

Customers who think the waitresses are offensive should see the manager

Don't even think of parking here

This is the wrong road to Dublin – do not take this road

The ten o'clock train left at half-nine and there will be no last train tonight. The rear portion of the train is not running and this train stops nowhere

The penny buns have been increased from 50p to 70p

This shop is closed on account of reopening

Ears pierced – pay for two and get one done free

Early closing day all day Wednesday

On a dance hall: *Ladies and gentlemen welcome regardless of sex*

Open 24 hours a day – longer at weekends

Disco on Sunday night. Very exclusive. Everybody welcome

In Cork's G.P.O.: *Pens will not be provided until people stop taking them away*

Notice in a Cork Hotel: *Please do not switch on the television except when in use*

Notice in Cork Golf Club: *Trousers may now be worn by ladies on the course – but they must be removed before entering the clubhouse*

Fine for parking here

Genuine antiques for sale – as new

On Cork jail at the turn on the century: *All prisoners not back in jail by 11pm sharp will be locked out for the night*

Do not come in this door – it is the entrance out

When this notice is under water it is unsafe to cross the river at this point

In a Cork auctioneers: *The highest bidder to be purchaser – unless somebody bids more*

It is our policy that no dissatisfied customer is ever allowed to leave this shop

Last petrol station until the next one

Visit our bargain basement on the third floor

Disarm today – dat arm tomorrow

On a Cork publisher's office door: *Gone to lunch – back in an hour. Already gone half an hour*

On an optician's window: *If you can't see what you want come inside at once – you may need spectacles*

On a laundry: *Why kill yourself with washing? Let us do it by hand*

There will be no trains running between Limerick and Cork on Sunday next and delays of up to thirty minutes can be expected

Beside an unofficial picket: *Business as usual during altercations*

Customers wanted – no previous experience necessary

On a Cork fish and chip shop: *We have a business arrangement with the local bank – they don't sell fish and chips and we don't cash cheques.*

A Cork traffic warden explained the system of yellow lines on city streets as follows: One yellow line means no parking at all. Two yellow lines means no parking at all at all.

***

Have you heard about the Corkman with an inferiority complex?

He thought that other people were nearly as good as he was.

***

What is the longest one-way street in the world?
The road from Cork to Dublin.

***

During the troubled times in Ireland a bunch of patriots attacked the country house of an Anglo-Irish landlord in West Cork. As they battered down the front door, they were met by an elegant and unflappable butler standing calmly at the bottom of the staircase. He announced, 'His Lordship is not at home'. They proceeded to ransack the building and set it on fire. As they left, the butler, still standing in the same place, enquired, 'Whom shall I say called, gentlemen?'

The following classic story, which I first heard from Frank Delaney, illustrates better than anything the subtlety of Cork humour.

There was a girl living in Cobh who fancied herself as a great beauty, put on airs and graces and generally behaved as if she was the bee's knees. One afternoon, dressed very provocatively she cycled past a group of workmen, hoping to impress them. As she passed by, one of the workmen said loudly to another, 'Nice bike, dough.'

***

Two Corkmen, who had never seen a tennis match were watching the Wimbledon ladies singles final between Chris Evert and Yvonne Goolagong on the television. After a while one of them said to the other, 'Goolagong, Goolagong, I wonder which Goolagong would she be now?'

***

A West Cork priest was preaching to his congregation in the last century. 'Drink is the cause of all your problems,' he thundered, 'it makes you angry, it makes you hate your landlords, it makes you shoot at your landlords and worst of all, it makes you miss them.'

Old Corkwomen are well-known for their down-to-earth attitude towards life, illness and the natural functions. The following is a conversation between two shawlies, shouted loudly at each other across Blarney Street.

'How is de husband, how is Mick today?'

'Fine tank God, fine tank God.'

'And how is his diarrhoea?'

'Tickenin, tank God, tickenin.'

***

A Corkman was in the casualty ward of a city hospital when he was visited by the Lady Mayoress.

'Now my good man,' she asked him, 'where were you injured?'

'In Washington Street,' he replied.

'No,' she said, 'in what part of the body?'

'Let me put it this way,' he said. 'If you had been injured where I was injured, you wouldn't have been injured at all.'

***

Corkmen love to tell Kerryman jokes. One of the most recent is the one about the two Kerrymen who were drowned in the Lee doing the Riverdance.

Here is a story that Corkmen like to tell. It's about a Bosnian footballer who signed for Limerick City football club. He became a big star and scored the winning goal in the cup final. So he rang his mother and said, 'Momma, I've become a big star and I scored the winning goal in the Cup final.'

'Don't talk to me about football,' said his mother, 'I've just been mugged, your sister has been raped, and your brother has been shot.'

'Well,' he said, 'it serves you right for coming to Limerick.'

***

In the old days of apartheid, a Corkman, well-known for his anti-apartheid views, was buying oranges in the city's covered English market. As the old lady was putting the oranges into a bag he asked her if the oranges came from South Africa.

'Yes they do, sir, they're the best South African oranges.'

'Put them back,' said the Corkman, 'I won't buy anything that comes from South Africa.'

'I don't blame you sir,' she said, 'all those blacks handling them.'

***

A Cork barman was closing up one night when he found a customer flat out under a table so he propped him up against the bar. When he turned round he found that the fellow had slid onto the floor again so he picked him up, searched his pockets and found his name and address. He lifted him outside and propped him up against his car while he opened the door, but the fellow slid onto the ground again. Finally, he got him into the car, drove him home and carried him up to the front door. To ring the doorbell he propped him up against the wall and found that he again slid down onto the ground. As he tried to lift him up again, the fellow's wife opened the door and said, 'Oh, thank goodness you've brought him home. But where is his wheelchair?'

***

Con and Jeremiah were out walking together when they saw a lorry passing by laden with grassy sods of earth for the laying of a lawn.

'Do you know Con,' said Jeremiah, 'if I ever win the Lotto, that's the first thing I'll have done – send away my lawn to be cut.'

***

It was said of a certain Corkman that he was very self-centred and always wanted to be the focus of attention. If he went to a funeral he would want to be the corpse.

Cork city has a famous covered market called the English Market, and there is a wide variety of meats, cheeses, fresh poultry and vegetables on sale there. In fact, there is an old Cork saying, 'take a stroll through the English Market and have your nostrils educated.'

In the English Market an American tourist once paid for a dozen oranges, but when he opened the bag he found only nine. When he brought this to the attention of the stall holder, she told him with a smile 'Yes, sir, three of them were bad, so I threw them away for you.'

***

The following announcement is reputed to have been made in a plane standing on the tarmac at Cork Airport.

Ladies and Gentlemen, sorry for the long delay in take off. I'm delighted to announce that we haven't got a bomb on board as we first feared. At least if we have, we haven't been able to find it.

In the penal times, there was a notice over the gates of the town of Bandon which read:

Jew or dissenter welcome here
but not a papist

Underneath, a local wag had written:

The man who wrote that wrote it well
for the same is writ o'er the gate of hell.

***

A Corkman wasn't feeling very well, so he went to the doctor to get some medicine.

'This is pretty strong stuff,' said the doctor, 'so take some the first day, then skip a day, then take some the third day, then skip a day and so on.'

A few weeks later the doctor met the man's wife and asked how he was.

'Oh he's dead,' she told him.

'Didn't the medicine I prescribed him do him any good?' asked the doctor.

'Oh the medicine was fine,' she replied, 'it was all that skipping that killed him.'

Soon after the Department of Agriculture introduced its premium bull scheme, a Cork farmer hired one of the best bulls in the country to service his cows. After nearly a month, the bull hadn't been returned, so the Department despatched an inspector hotfoot to Cork to see what the situation was. He found the bull pulling a plough round a field, the Cork farmer whipping him along and shouting, 'Get along outa that, ye bugger ye, that'll teach you there's more to life than romance.'

***

A Corkman was asked to give his opinion of Kerry hurling. He said it reminded him of some form of compulsory tillage.

***

A Corkman lay dying in a Dublin hospital in the 1940s. A telegram was sent to his brother in Cork to come immediately before it was too late. Because of the war, there was a petrol shortage, so the brother in Cork cycled all the way up to Dublin, took his bicycle up three flights of stairs and into the patient's room. Once in, he let the air out of both tyres. When the Corkman got one whiff of the pure Cork air, he recovered at once, and do you know what I'm going to tell you, that man is still alive and in a state of perfect health.

A Corkman was the oldest man in Ireland and had reached the remarkable age of a hundred and twenty years. The *Examiner* sent their top reporter to interview him on the occasion of his birthday.

'To what do you attribute your great age?' the reporter asked him.

'To the fact that it is so long since I was born,' he replied.

'Be serious,' said the reporter, 'how have you managed to live to a hundred and twenty?'

'Vitamin pills,' said the Corkman. 'I've been taking them every day since I was a hundred and ten.'

***

The great Cork writer Seán O'Faolain once described an Irish queer as a fellow who preferred women to drink.

***

How many Cork City councillors does it take to change a light bulb?

Twenty-five – one to change the light bulb and twenty-four to see how they do it in Florida.

***

A tourist passing through Cork had an emergency late one night so he asked the first person he met if Cork had any 24 hour chemist shops.

'We have half-a-dozen of them,' said the obliging Corkman.

'Well can you direct me to the nearest one?' asked the tourist urgently.

'Aah there would be no point doing that,' said the Corkman, 'sure they'd all be closed at this hour of the night.'

***

The following road sign, intended for heavy lorries crossing a Cork bridge, was unfortunately placed adjacent to a public toilet: *Limit two tons*

***

A little West Cork village had two hotels so a tourist asked a local man which of the two of them provided the better accommodation.

'Let me put it this way,' said the Corkman, 'which ever of them you stay at you'll be sorry you didn't stay at the other one.'

***

A woman applied for a job as a roadsweeper with Cork Corporation, but the foreman was a bit doubtful about employing her.

'Look,' he said to her, 'I don't think you'd be up to the rigours of the job.'

'Give me that brush and let me show you,' she said, and proceeded to give a perfect demonstration of how to sweep a road.

'Right, you're on,' said the foreman, 'report for work at ten o'clock next Monday morning.'

'But I thought Corporation workmen started work at eight o'clock in the morning.'

'That's true,' said the foreman, 'but for the first two hours they just stand around scratching their balls.'

***

***

What does CAD stand for?
Cork Dyslexia Association.

***

Have you heard about the Corkman who does wonderful work for local hospitals?
He makes people sick.

Con wrote the following letter to his ex-girlfriend.

Dear Mary,

I haven't been able to get a wink of sleep since we broke up. I think of you all the time, only you, and nobody else can ever replace you in my heart. Can we try again to make things work? You are the love of my life for ever and ever.

Your darling Con.

P.S. Congratulations on winning the National Lottery.

***

'That little lad looks over fourteen to me,' said a Cork bus conductor to a lady seeking half fare for her boy on the bus.

'How could he be, and me only married ten years?' she replied.

'Look lady,' said the conductor, 'I'm just collecting fares, not hearing confessions.'

***

Have you ever been in a Cork bus queue? One theory is that a Cork queue is descended from a group of brigands who would assemble to rob the passengers of incoming coaches in previous generations. It hasn't changed much.

A Cork bride wanted to get married on a Friday in June, but the bridegroom insisted on getting married on a Thursday. He explained to her – 'if we get married on a Friday, our silver wedding anniversary will fall on a Monday and Monday evening is my bowling evening.'

***

A true story told to me by a Cork priest. A man in his parish drank three pints of Murphy's stout religiously every day. When the priest asked him what he was doing for Lent, he told him that he was giving up his daily three pints of Murphy's and as an additional punishment he was going to drink three pints of Guinness instead.

***

This fellow went into a bar and there was a Corkman beside the biggest dog he had ever seen.

'Does your dog bite sir?' he asked the Corkman.

'No,' said the Corkman, 'my dog is as gentle as a lamb.'

So the fellow went over and patted the dog and the dog nearly bit his arm off.

'I thought you told me your dog didn't bite,' he screamed at the Corkman.

'That's right,' said the Corkman, 'but that's not my dog.'

Cork had its own band of fighting men officially known as the Cork Militia. It was said of the Cork Militia that they were useless in times of war and dangerous in times of peace.

***

In Cork, premature ejaculation is having to go to the toilet after only your fifth pint.

***

The famous parliamentarian Tim Healy once asked an elderly Parish Priest why there were no Jesuits in the diocese of Cork.

'I attribute that Mr Healy,' he replied, 'to the power of prayer.'

***

Underneath the impressive Calvary scene in a Cork graveyard the following notice stood for many years:

Executed by Neff Brothers of Cork

***

Con's wife was having a baby so he rang the maternity hospital.

'Is this her first baby?' asked the nurse.

'No,' said Con, 'this is her husband speaking.'

***

Shamus O'Shamus in his book on Ireland has the following tongue-in-cheek description of Cork:

> Cork, like Dublin, possesses a river, but there is no record that any Cork townsman has ever succeeded in spitting across it. That is not to say that the townsmen of Cork have given up trying. Indeed, some Cork townsmen endeavour to keep themselves in practice even when their beautiful river is not in sight.

***

Two Corkmen in the last century were waiting in ambush for their landlord, their sworn enemy with a view to terminating his landlordship. As they waited in a cold, wet ditch hour after hour, one of them suddenly said to the other, 'He's late. I hope to God nothing has happened to the poor fellow.'

Two Corkman joined the RAF during the Second World War. As they flew their bomber over Berlin with anti-aircraft fire and shells bursting all around them one of them suddenly shouted out 'Hurrah for De Valera'.

'Why are you shouting out "Hurrah for De Valera" at this particular point in time?' asked the other.

'Why wouldn't I?' said the first Corkman, 'wasn't it him kept us out of the war?'

***

There was a huge crowd in Cork's City Hall recently at the concert given by Teresa Pranos.

***

Cork politeness and deference to rank are legendary. An eminent friend of mine once found himself standing in the urinal of the Imperial Hotel next to a gentleman engaged in the same activity.

'Are you who I think you are?' he asked.

'Yes,' replied my friend smiling.

'I thought that all right; excuse me now talking to you with this in me hand.'

***

$\mathbf{A}$ Cork international rugby player, a fine cut of a lad admittedly, had a devoted following of young female fans who attended all his matches and pestered him for autographs and personal effects such as sweaty jock-straps and locks of his hair. One of these lassies, a bit bolder than the others, asked him a rather personal and intimate question.

'Are we to assume,' she inquired coyly, 'that you are built proportionately in all parts of your body?'

'Jaysus,' he said to her, 'if I was built proportionately, I'd be eight foot six.'

***

$\mathbf{A}$ Dubliner, a Corkman and a Kerryman each tendered to a government official for a big construction job.

'I'll do it for £200,000,' said the Kerryman.

'How is that figure broken down?' asked the official.

'£100,000 for materials and £100,000 for labour,' said the Kerryman.

'I'll do it for £400,000,' said the Dubliner, 'that's £200,000 for materials and £200,000 for labour.'

'Look,' said the Corkman, 'my tender is for £600,000. That's £200,000 for you, £200,000 for me, and we'll give the remaining £200,000 to the Kerryman to do the job.'

***

What does a Cork shopkeeper say to a German tourist? God bless the mark.

***

Have you heard about the Corkman who had two wooden legs?

A fire broke out and he was burned to the ground. He applied to the insurance company for compensation, but they told him that he hadn't a leg to stand on.

***

Jeremiah and his wife were watching Cork's annual military parade of men who had taken part in the fight for freedom.

'Isn't it wonderful,' said Jeremiah, 'to see all the men who died for Ireland marching by?'

***

An American woman in a Cork post office was upset about the long queue so when she saw a man arriving at another window, rushed over to form a queue.

'I'm not here at all, ma'am, ' he told her, 'and the fellow who is here isn't here either.'

NIALL TÓIBÍN

One of Cork's greatest contributions to humour is the much-loved comedian Niall Tóibín. He is a superb mimic, blessed with the gift of perfect timing, and with the late Jimmy O'Dea can be ranked as one of the greatest comedians that Ireland has ever produced, and that is no small claim to fame. Tóibín has a particular insight into the Cork character and most of his stories about Cork put their finger on the spot unerringly, so much so that one suspects that in his heart and soul he has never left 'de banks' behind. Here are just a few of the master's best Cork stories, told in his language:

An aged and dear friend of mine who travelled the country a great deal but always tried to get back for the 'Barrs' important games, collapsed on his way from the altar one Sunday morning. At his wake someone murmured something to the effect that poor Tim was gone.

'What d'ye mean "poor" Tim?' came the rebuke. 'Didn't he die at the Mass the year that the 'Barrs beat the Glen?'

One of Niall Tóibín's favourite stories about Cork refers to a man who mentioned in a pub a news item from 'de paper' concerning a Russian agent who defecated to the West.

There is one conversational ploy I have come across time and again in Cork which I have not experienced elsewhere, certainly not handled with the same clinical finesse. It consists in getting the stranger to concur in a series of totally unexceptionable statements or sentiments and then skewering him to the wall with a barb of contempt. A couple of examples:

A friend of mine was accosted by one whose hopes of attaining high office in a certain musical foundation had been dashed by the appointment of a mutual acquaintance.

'God, isn't it great to see Ned getting on so well?'

'It is, God knows.'

'Of course he put in the time. Done the work. Still isn't it a great honour all the same.'

'Oh, there's no doubt. What you might call I suppose the peak of musical achievement, really.'

'Yes.' Pause.

'Come 'ere to me, he can barely recognise the National Anthem.'

The Northside and Southside of Cork city never confront each other more dramatically than when their respective hurling clubs Glen Rovers (De Glin) and St Finbarr's (De Barrs) meet in combat. A story is told of two Glen supporters going astray on their way home after a crushing defeat by the Barrs. They pause on the South Gate Bridge and disconsolately shy the remnants of their sandwiches at the swans. Suddenly one asks 'Where are we?'

'On the South Gate Bridge.'

'The South Gate Bridge?'

'Come on outa that. We'll go up to the North Gate Bridge and feed our own swans!'

I used to go into a pub where there was a sing-song every night and there was a man called Bill who had more or less elected himself permanent MC of this sing-song. One night he called me over and said to me, 'The boys are all dying for me to sing, but I can't call on myself to, because I'm the MC and that would be very bad form. But I'll tell you what I'll do, I'll call on you to sing, and you sing your song, and you do your encore, because I'll make sure that they give you an encore, you needn't worry about that at all. And then you say that you have a very special request for me to sing.

'So I'll say "all right, what do I want you to sing?"

'You want me to sing by special request the Bando-lero from *Trial by Jury*.'

So I sang my song and I did my encore and then I got up and I said 'now lads I have a very special request, I want Bill to sing for me the Bandolero from *Trial by Jury*.'

So he looked over at me and said 'I don't know Niall, I think that would be a bit above their heads.' And then he looked at them and said 'Sure we all know the Bandolero is not from *Trial by Jury* at all.'

After the *Titanic* sank, there were many people gathered in the harbour at Cobh anxiously awaiting news of their loved ones who had sailed on the ship's fateful maiden voyage.

However there was also a polar bear there and he whispered anxiously to a policeman 'Is there any news of the iceberg?'

***

A Corkman was talking about the hard times when he was a boy.

'All my clothes were bought at the Army and Navy stores,' he told his audience. 'I had to go to school dressed as a Japanese admiral.'

***

At a concert in West Cork, the Parish Priest was asked to act as MC and he gladly agreed. The concert was going very well and it came to the final act of the night.

'Maggie Murphy,' said the Parish Priest, 'will now bring the proceedings to a close with a fine old Irish ballad.'

A voice from back of the hall rang out 'Maggie Murphy is nothing but a fat ould hoor.'

'Nevertheless,' said the Parish Priest.

***

Cork's famous Shandon Bells are known far and wide in verse and reality. Maybe not so well-known is the following verse:

The Bells of Shandon sound so grand on

The lovely waters of the Lee

But the Bells of St Nicholas

Sound so ridiculous

On the dirty waters

Of Sullivan's Quay.

***

Con was asked in a quiz how to walk from Bishopstown to Mayfield without passing a single pub. He said, 'Go into all of them'.

A Corkman was dreaming all night of the number seven. Then next morning he woke up at seven minutes past seven and noticed that there was a horse called 'Seven' running in the seventh race at the Curragh (seven letters in that) and the odds were seven to one. So he put seven hundred and seventy seven pounds on the horse and the horse came in seventh.

***

In centuries gone by, Cork's Butter Market was justly famous. It is said that when Stanley was exploring Central Africa, searching for Livingstone, in the middle of the dense jungle, he came across a box with *Cork Butter Market* written on it.

***

Con and Jeremiah were travelling on the train from Cork to Cobh when a well-endowed woman sitting opposite them started to breastfeed her baby.

'What is she doing?' Jeremiah asked Con.

'Will you be quiet,' said Con, 'she is only feeding the baby.'

'He's not going to eat all that is he?' said Jeremiah.

The baby was reluctant to feed, however. Its mother coaxed it by saying 'if you don't take that now, I'm going to give it to the man.'

A pilot and his co-pilot were coming in to land at Cork Airport. On their first approach they overshot the runway and had to take the aircraft back up again and circle the airport. This happened a second time, but at the third attempt with a superhuman effort, the plane was brought to a halt.

'Do you know,' said the pilot, 'that's the shortest runway I've ever come across.'

'And it's the widest one I've ever come across,' said the co-pilot.

***

A Corkwoman went to her lawyer and told him that she wanted a separation from her husband.

'On what grounds?' asked the lawyer.

'Why here in Cork,' said the woman.

'No, no,' said the lawyer, 'do you have a grudge?'

'Yes, we have a double grudge because we have two cars.'

'No, no, no,' said the lawyer, 'does he ever beat you up?'

'No, I always get up at seven, and he doesn't get up until eight.'

'Look,' said the lawyer in desperation, 'why do you want a separation?'

'We seem to have difficulty communicating,' said the Corkwoman.

A well-known Cork character had been separated from his parents when he was a child and had assumed that they were both dead. To his amazement, they were both discovered, alive and well, in an old folks home. His first action on learning this was to hurry down to the Dominicans in Popes Quay and demand back all the money he had paid for masses for them over the years.

***

Con and Jeremiah, two keen anglers on the Lough in Cork, were having a competition to see which of them could tell the biggest lie.

'I once caught a fish in the Lough,' said Con, 'and it was so big, its picture alone weighed twenty pounds.'

'I can top that,' said Jeremiah. 'I once caught a fish in the Lough, and it was so big that when I took it out, the level of the Lough fell by six feet.'

***

Cork's Silicon Valley is one of the most important contributions to Ireland's fast developing micro-electronics industry. Cork's main claim to fame is that it manufactures the world's biggest microchip.

***

Town and Gown

Queen's College, Cork, founded in 1845 with about a hundred students, has grown into University College, Cork with over ten thousand students and a thousand staff. College has always occupied a special place in the hearts of the people of Cork and Munster, but they are not above making the odd joke about my beloved institution.

A first class honours engineering graduate of UCC got a big job in a factory. On his first morning at work the foreman handed him a brush and said 'sweep the floor'.

'Hold on,' said the fellow, 'I'm a first class honours graduate of UCC.'

'That's all right,' said the foreman, 'I'll show you how to do it.'

What do you say to a UCC arts graduate with a job? Big Mac and fries please.

'Mummy, Mummy, Mummy can I play with my dolls' house?'

'No, certainly not. You know very well I've just let it to six UCC students.'

An extract from a UCC sociology lecture: Here is a list of statistics of West Cork farmers broken down by age and sex.

Voice at the back: Professor, what about the drink?

Why is a UCC professor like a lighthouse in the middle of a bog?

They are both brilliant but useless.

A young UCC commerce student got a job with the *Cork Examiner* and his first job was collecting accounts in Mayfield. He knocked on a door which was opened with the traditional greeting, 'What's wrong with ya?'

'Well it's about a little bill you have overdue at the *Examiner*,' said our hero, brandishing his account book.

'Show, give me a look at that, I don't owe the *Examiner* nothing at all.'

'Yes it says here clearly, three pounds for a lost and found ad when your dog disappeared.'

'Aah,' said the Mayfield man, 'I don't owe you a penny because that dog came home on its own.'

What do a UCC poet and William Shakespeare have in common?

Neither has written a decent poem in the last 300 years.

In the 1930s there was a medical professor with a slight stammer teaching at UCC. One day he was lecturing about the human excretory system when a female medical student began to giggle.

'Look,' he said to her, 'it may be just ssshit to you, but it's my bread and butter.'

An eminent Corkman was telling his friends about his private audience with the Pope during a recent visit to Rome.

'He asked me if I had any children,' he told his impressed listeners, 'and I told him I had five, and then he asked me what the eldest was doing, so I told him he was doing Electrical Engineering at UCC.'

'And what did the Pope say to that?' they asked him.

'Dat's the comin ting,' said the Pope, 'dat's the comin ting,' he replied.

***

Con's wife was in hospital having a baby so he rang the Maternity hospital to see how she was getting on. Unfortunately he dialled the wrong number and was put through to the Cork Cricket Club instead.

'What's the position?' he asked the man who answered the phone.

'Well,' said the man, 'we have seven of them out now and we hope to have the rest out before tea. The last three were ducks.'

***

A Cork woman was boasting to the neighbours about her son.

'He's one of the cleverest and most obliging lads in the country,' she told them, 'he's always helping the police with their inquiries.'

***

A Texan visiting Cork asked his guide to show him the biggest building in Cork and when he did the Texan said 'Is that it? Why back in Texas we have buildings a thousand times bigger than that.'

'I'm not surprised.' said the Corkman, 'That's the local lunatic asylum.'

Con and Jeremiah were on a trip to Rome and were wandering around in the Pope's private garden. Suddenly, they saw the Pope slip down some steps and crack his skull on the marble floor.

'The Pope is a goner,' said Jeremiah, 'but they will hush things up for a few days. Let's get back to Cork and we will get terrific odds at the bookies on the Pope dying in the next few days.'

So back home they went, borrowed all the money they could and Con visited all the bookies in Cork.

A few days later, right enough, the Pope died. Jeremiah phoned Con and said, 'We're in the money.'

'Unfortunately not,' replied Con, 'I did a double with the Pope and the Archbishop of Dublin.'

***

A new young horticultural instructor was appointed to West Cork and was doing a tour of the place. He found one old farmer in his orchard and he began to lay down the law about his out of date methods for fruit growing.

'Look at this tree,' he said, 'it's not properly pruned, not properly fertilised and it's planted in the wrong place. I'd be surprised if you get ten pounds of apples off that tree.'

'So would I,' said the Corkman, 'that's a bloody pear tree.'

A police inspector from Dublin was appointed as the new police inspector for West Cork so a few weeks before his appointment was officially announced he decided to pay a visit to West Cork, incognito and in plain clothes, to see the lie of the land in his new constituency. Wandering around a West Cork village at midnight one night he met the local guard and asked him if he knew of any pub where he could get a drink after hours.

'I'll look after you,' said the guard, 'sure the pubs don't close here until mid-October.'

At about four o'clock in the morning, as the carousing was continuing, he said to the guard 'What would your sergeant say if he could see you now?'

The guard looked at him with a sly wink.

'He'd say wasn't I the cute hoor to be drinking with the new inspector.'

***

A Corkman arrived at the gates of Heaven and was asked by St Peter where he was from.

'I'm from Cork,' he said proudly.

'Get to Hell out of here,' said St Peter, 'surely you don't expect us to cook tripe and drisheen for one?'

***

A tour bus was travelling around places of interest in Cork county. As they neared Kinsale, the driver said, 'This is Kinsale where the Irish had a decisive victory over the English.' As they passed Bantry, the driver said, 'This is Bantry where the Irish Army hammered the English army on numerous occasions.'

An English tourist was a bit fed up of this, so he said, 'Surely the English defeated the Irish in some battles?'

'Not on this bus they didn't,' said the driver.

***

A Corkman on a business trip to London finished his business rather more quickly than he expected, so he took an early flight home to surprise the family. He phoned home to ask his wife to come to the airport to collect him. When a little boy answered the phone, he said to him, 'Son get your mother to come to the phone.'

'I can't dad,' said the little boy, 'she's upstairs in bed with the milkman.'

'What,' said the man, 'look son, get my shotgun from under the stairs, load it and let both of them have it.'

A few minutes later the boy came back and said, 'I did what you told me dad – they tried to jump out the window but I shot them as they jumped. They are both dead and floating face down on the swimming pool.'

'What swimming pool?' said the Corkman, 'we don't have a swimming pool. Is this Cork 1234567?'

Con was working for the corporation in Cork sweeping out the public toilets and doing a terrific job. Then an order came down from Dublin that all public service employees had to take a written examination to hold on to their jobs. Poor Con, who could neither read nor write, lost his job. He emigrated to America and opened a paper stall in New York and did very well. He next bought a little shop and in a short time prospered so much that he opened a chain of newsagents stores all across America. Soon he was a billionaire and one night he appeared on television to present a million dollar cheque to charity.

'Now if you will just sign here sir,' said the TV presenter.

'I'm sorry,' said Con, 'I can't read or write.'

'Can't read or write,' said the presenter, 'where would you be today if you could read and write?'

'Back in Cork,' smiled Con, 'cleaning out shit houses.'

***

What do you need if you find three Cork lawyers up their necks in cement?

More cement.

***

Two Corkmen were arrested for fighting and appeared before the court.

'We weren't fighting, your honour,' said one of them.

'What were you doing then?' the judge asked.

'We were trying to separate each other,' the second told him.

***

A woman got on a number eight bus in Patrick Street and asked the driver to let her know when they had reached the Bishopstown Shopping Centre.

At every stop she asked him, 'Is this the Bishopstown Shopping Centre?' and he replied as politely as he could that it was not.

Finally she asked, 'Driver, how am I going to know when we have reached the Bishopstown Shopping Centre?'

'By the big smile on my face, lady,' he told her.

CORK LEGAL STORIES

Cork is legendary for its legal anecdotes and stories. Maurice Healy wrote a whole book of them – *The Old Munster Circuit*. Here are some of the funniest stories from the courts of Cork that I have collected over the years. Doubtless, there are a thousand others.

Cork's most notorious wino and drunkard was before the court for the umpteenth time charged with being drunk and disorderly. He already had three hundred and sixty-five previous convictions for the same offence. He was red-eyed, ragged and torn and he threw himself at the mercy of the court.

'Right,' said the judge, 'I'm going to give you a suspended sentence, although normally I send people to jail in cases like this. It appears to me that all your troubles stem from drink, so I want you to give me your solemn promise that you will never touch a drop of alcohol again as long as you live. Not even the teensiest weensiest sherry before luncheon.'

A Cork lawyer pleaded on behalf of his client: Consider the defendant's mother, his only mother.

Another Cork lawyer whose client was charged with murdering his father and mother by cutting their heads off with an axe, opened his defence as follows: Gentleman of the jury, consider my client, recently orphaned.

'Why did you steal nearly half a million pounds?' the judge asked a Cork businessman.

'I was hungry, your honour,' was the reply.

'You are discharged,' said the judge, 'and allowed to leave the court with no other stain on your character other than the fact that you have been found not guilty by a Cork jury.'

During a murder trial in Cork in the nineteenth century there was a sensation when the man who was supposed to have been murdered actually turned up in the courtroom. The judge immediately ordered the jury to return a verdict of 'not guilty'. After several hours deliberating the jury returned and the foreman announced that they had found the defendant guilty.

'How on earth could you reach such a verdict,' asked the judge, 'when the murdered man is here in court?'

'Yes, we know that your honour,' answered the foreman, 'but a few of us have grounds to believe that the defendant is the man who stole my brother's horse a few years ago.'

A Cork woman was charged with driving at eighty miles an hour down the middle of the road. In defence, she stated that one of the instructions on her driving test application form had been 'tear along the dotted line'.

A Corkman who was fined £50 for being drunk and disorderly told the judge that he had no money to pay the fine.

'You would if you hadn't spent it on drink,' the judge told him.

A West Cork man was in court charged with stealing a horse.

'You have a choice,' the judge told him. 'You can be tried by me alone, or by a jury of your peers.

'What do mean by "peers"?' he asked.

'Peers are your equals, men of your own kind and class,' said the judge.

'Try me yourself,' said the West Cork man, 'I don't want to be tried by a bunch of horse thieves.

A Corkman was up in court charged with a very serious offence.

'Do you plead guilty or not guilty?' asked the judge.

'What else have you got?' asked the Corkman.

A Corkman was charged with murder but was acquitted by the skin of his teeth. After the trial he told his lawyer that he could prove he was innocent because he was in jail at the time when the crime was committed.

'Why on earth didn't you tell that to the court?' asked his astonished lawyer.

'I thought it might prejudice the jury against me,' said the Corkman.

A Corkman was up in court charged with a very serious offence.

Judge: The jury have found you guilty.

Corkman: I know they have your honour but I'm sure your honour has too much intelligence to pay any attention to what a shower of rogues like that have to say.

A Corkman had been found guilty of a serious crime and the judge asked him if he could pay anything at all towards the huge fine and costs against him.

'Not a penny, your honour,' he replied. 'Everything I own I've given to my lawyer and three of the jury.'

A Corkman was up in Court charged with riding a bicycle with no light on.

'How do you plead?' the judge asked him.

'Guilty, your honour,' said the Corkman, 'but insane.'

District Justice: Who is appearing for you, my man?

Corkman: I'm conducting my own case, your honour.

District Justice: Are you pleading guilty or not guilty?

Corkman: Not guilty. Sure if I was guilty, I'd have a lawyer, your honour.

A Corkwoman was giving evidence at a trial where her husband was accused of burglary. She was being cross-examined by a rather haughty prosecuting council.

'Is it true,' he asked her, 'that when you were getting married, you actually knew that your husband was a burglar?'

'That is true,' she replied.

'And can you give the court any possible reason why you would want to marry a man you knew was a burglar?'

'Well,' she replied, 'I had a choice between a burglar and a lawyer, so I married the burglar.'

'No further questions, Your honour.'

A Corkman in court was asked by the judge why he had no counsel to defend him.

'I don't need one, your honour,' he replied with a twinkle in his eye, 'because I have some very good friends on the jury.'

Lawyer: Do you wish to challenge any member of the jury?

Corkman: I think I could fight that little fellow on the end.

A Corkwoman in court charged with driving down a street clearly marked *No Access* pleaded in defence that her card was a *Visa*.

'Is religion involved in any way in this case?' the judge asked the defence counsel.

'No, my lord,' he answered, 'all the parties involved are Presbyterian.'

SOME CORK JURY VERDICTS

We find the defendant guilty as charged. We admit he didn't do it as he was somewhere else at the time, but we are sure he would have done it if he got the chance.

We find the man who stole the horse not guilty.

We are all of one mind – insane.

We are unanimous, nine to three.

Not guilty, if he promises to emigrate.

We the jury would have given anything to have been present at this fight.

We the jury are of the unanimous opinion that we require another barrel of porter before we can reach a verdict.

Foreman of the jury: We cannot reach a verdict until I get those eleven stubborn brutes to change their minds.

A little Corkman no more than four feet six in height was sitting on a bus when the driver had to brake suddenly. The little fellow was thrown forward from his seat and landed with a crash in the aisle. A well-meaning woman rushed to help him and pick him up but he was a grumpy fellow and told her in no uncertain terms to mind her own business and leave him alone and that he was perfectly capable of looking after himself. So he brushed himself down and resumed his seat.

However, as he got off the bus, the woman shouted after him, 'When you get home, I hope Snow White kicks the hell out of you.'

***

When Con died it was remarked that he had spent nearly all his life lying in bed looking for work. His widow had him cremated and put some of his ashes in an hour glass. As she turned it upside down she said with some satisfaction, 'There at last you're doing a bit of work about the house.'

***

Jeremiah's wife used to carry a lock of her husband's hair in a locket around her neck in memory of her husband. When a friend remarked that Jeremiah was still with us, she replied, 'I know that, but his hair is all gone.'

Corkwoman: Doctor, is there any hope at all for my husband?

Doctor: Very little, but I've knocked the fever out of him and you'll have the consolation of knowing he died cured.

Corkwoman: Well thank God he's not dying of anything serious.

***

This true story was told to me by a Cork travel agent. He was conducting a tour by bus in the Holy Land when the bus was stopped by two United Nations soldiers whose jeep had broken down in dangerous country. They asked if they could have a lift back to camp which was just a few miles up the road. The soldiers turned out to be Irish, better still from Cork, and one of them announced, 'I'm from Blackpool'. A lady's voice from the back of the bus rang out, 'Well you're on the wrong bus. This one is going to Knocknaheeney.'

***

The weather in Cork is something else. It's the only place in the world you can wake up in the morning and hear the birds coughing.

***

Two Cork girls, Imelda and Attracta, were attending a sex-education class.

'Attracta, did you understand all that?'

'Every word of it, Imelda. What's on your mind?'

'Tell me, Attracta, are you a virgin?'

'Oh no, Imelda, not yet.'

***

The general manager of a large banking group was travelling around the country incognito checking up on the efficiency of his branches. He came to a little branch in West Cork where the bank was closed during banking hours and three staff were playing poker with the bank's money. To give them a fright, he rang the alarm bell three times but none of them moved. However, a few minutes later the barman from the pub across the road brought over three pints of stout.

***

A well-known Cork T.D. sends the following reply to all the abusive letters he receives:

Dear Sir,

I have been receiving letters from a mentally disturbed person who is using your name. I thought you would like to know.

A Corkman was an undertaker and one day a wealthy young woman came into his premises and identified a corpse as that of her father. She gave orders for an expensive and elaborate funeral. Just as she was about to leave, the corpse's lower jaw opened and exposed a set of false teeth.

'My father didn't have false teeth,' she shrieked, 'cancel that order.'

The Cork undertaker took the body out of the expensive coffin and said to it, 'You fool, you'd have had a first class funeral if only you'd kept your damn mouth shut.'

***

Inscription on a doctor's tombstone in a Cork cemetery

If you want to see my memorial look around you.

***

Con was working on the Cork-Limerick railway, when suddenly a train came speeding along the line. Con took off down the track but was knocked down and badly injured. When he regained consciousness in hospital, the doctor asked him why he had not run up the embankment.

'Don't be a fool,' said Con. 'If I couldn't outrun it on the flat, what chance had I running uphill?'

$\mathbf{A}$ Cork Southside politician was canvassing on the Northside of the city during a by-election, and he was a bit out of his depth. When he knocked on a door and it was opened by a woman with a scantily clad baby in her arms, he didn't know what to do. Should he kiss the baby or just praise it?

'That's a fine child you have there, mam,' he said to her, 'tell me, can he talk?'

'Can he talk, can he talk?' she said back to him, 'Cornelius say "fuck" for the gentleman.'

***

'**W**hat have you got in your pocket?' Con asked Jeremiah.

'I'll give you a clue,' said Jeremiah. 'It begins with the letter N.'

'A napple,' said Con.

'No,' said Jeremiah, 'I told you that it begins with the letter N.'

'How about a norange?' said Con.

'No, no,' said Jeremiah, 'I'm telling you for last time that it begins with an N.'

'Would it be a nonion?' asked Con in desperation.

'You got it at last,' said Jeremiah.

***

Con went to New York and was driving round in a cab and the cab driver asked him the following riddle – Who has the same father and mother as me but is not my brother and not my sister?

'I don't know,' said Con.

'It's me,' said the cab driver.

'That's a good one,' said Con to himself, 'I must tell that one to the lads when I get home.'

So one night in the pub he asked his friends, 'Who has the same father and mother as me, but is not my brother or my sister?'

'We give up,' they said after some deliberation.

'It's a cab driver in New York,' said Con.

***

A Cork couple had seventeen children so the Vatican decided to present them with a gold medal struck specially in their honour. The Papal Nuncio delivered the medal in person and told them they were a credit to the Catholic Church.

'There must be some mistake,' they told him, 'we're not Catholics.'

'Oh my God,' said the Papal Nuncio, 'don't tell me we've minted a gold medal for two sex-crazy Protestants.'

***

SOME CORK SAYINGS

Is the new baby a boy or a child?

Very changeable weather isn't it? You wouldn't know what to pawn.

On being served Brussels sprouts: You've made a balls of the cabbage again.

How am I? 'Tis only barely overground I am.

On being invited to a cremation: What time are they setting the match to Mick?

It has to be true – I read it in de paper.

By a fellow with his arms around you: Come 'ere to me boy, do you know what I'm going to tell you?

Are you reading that newspaper you're sitting on?

Is it yourself that's in it?

He kissed me like a cow's foot coming up out of a bog-hole.

Con was taking his driving test and to the examiner's amazement he went straight through a red light.

'Why did you do that?' he asked Con, 'we might have been killed.'

'Not to worry,' grinned Con, 'the brother, who's an expert driver, told me to drive through the red – he's being doing it for years and has never had an accident.'

A couple of minutes later Con drove straight through another red light.

'Look,' screamed the examiner, 'you really are trying to kill me.'

Then they came to a green light and Con slammed on the brakes, nearly sending the examiner through the wind-screen.

'What the heck did you do that for?' he roared.

'I always stop when the lights are green,' explained Con, 'after all, the brother might be coming the other way.'

***

A very popular Corkman died in the early 1930s and a tremendous wake got into full swing. When the undertaker called to collect the body with his traditional inquiry of, 'Is this where the man that's dead lives?' the widow of the dead man asked him if he would ever mind calling back in a few days as the wake was going so well.

'We have to be sure he's really dead,' she said 'and not just dead drunk.'

***

During a recent trawl of the Atlantic floor of the coast of Cork, local archaeologists recovered the wheel of a horse cart. They concluded that Corkmen were going to America by road before the flood.

***

Jeremiah's marriage was a stormy one but when he died, his widow, just to keep up appearances, mourned him in the traditional manner. When a neighbour called to pay his respects he held the corpse's hand and suddenly said to her, 'Hold on, I wonder if he's dead at all, because his hand still feels hot to me.'

The widow looked him straight in the eye and said, 'Hot or cold, out that door he goes at seven o'clock this evening.'

A Corkman was marooned on a desert island for many years with no hope of rescue. One day he found a bottle in the sand and when he picked it up and rubbed it, out popped a genie.

'Thank heavens you've rescued me,' said the genie, 'I was stuck in that bottle for over two thousand years.' He was just about to depart when the Corkman said, 'Hey, what about my reward?'

The genie just pointed a finger at him and said, 'You will be lucky,' and vanished.

Right enough, the very next day, the Corkman was rescued and brought home by jumbo jet. As he was walking down Patrick's Street he found a twenty pound note on the ground, so he picked it up and popped into a bookies shop where he spotted a horse called Desert Isle running at a hundred to one, so he put the lot on him. The horse romped home. In the next race there was a horse called Genie so he put all his winnings on him again at a hundred to one and the horse romped home. In the final race was a horse called Lucky Sailor so he put the lot on him and he romped home too at a hundred to one. So on his first day back home he was a millionaire. He booked a top hotel and had a slap-up meal. 'Can I get you anything else sir?' asked the manager. 'Yes,' said the Corkman, 'I would like the company for the night of a beautiful Indian princess complete with sari and spot on her forehead.' This was done, and as the Princess slept in his arms he idly began to pick at the spot on her forehead until he actually removed it. Underneath he found the words 'You have won a car'.

***

A woman went into Roche's Stores in Cork and asked the floorwalker if he kept stationary.

'No, madam,' he replied, 'if I did that I'd lose my job.'

***

The definition of a Cork intellectual is a man who visits the Crawford Art Gallery even when it's not raining!

***

Con, a bit the worse for drink, lay sitting on the ground, confused as it were.

'Where am I?' he asked a passing lady.

'You're at the corner of Washington Street and the Grand Parade,' she told him courteously.

'Cut the details,' said Con, 'what city?'

***

Con's doctor has told him to take more exercise. He's thinking of rolling his own cigarettes.

93

There was a discussion in a Cork pub one night as to who was the greatest man who had ever lived. One man claimed it was Jesus Christ, another Michael Collins, a third Christy Ring, and a fourth Jack Lynch. Finally, a little man sipping his pint stated categorically, 'The greatest man who ever lived was a man by the name of Patrick Alphonsus Murphy.'

'How come none of us ever heard of him?' asked the other, 'who was he exactly?'

'Gentlemen,' he replied, 'he was my wife's first husband.'

**

The Parish Priest in a Cork church was amazed to see a woman doing the Stations of the Cross starting at the fourteenth and working her way backwards.

'That's not the way to do it,' he said to her, 'you've go to start at number one and go forwards.'

'I thought there was something wrong all right,' said the lady. 'He seemed to be getting better.'

**

You can always know when summer is approaching in Cork. The rain gets warmer.

A tourist was standing in the middle of Cork's Patrick Street a bit lost. So she asked a kindly CIE (Courtesy In Everything) man, 'If I stand where I am, will I get the bus to Douglas?'

'Look missus,' he said to her , 'If you stand where you are now, you'll get the bus for Douglas right in the middle of your arse.'

***

A foreign passenger at Mallow railway station consulted his timetable, only to find that his train was over three hours late. He attacked an innocent porter standing around with the words, 'I don't know why you people have a timetable at all.'

The porter eyed him coolly and retorted, 'If we did not have a timetable, how would we know how late the train was?'

***

Another American tourist in a hotel bar didn't find Cork to his liking and made no secret of the fact.

'This Cork is the pits,' he said to the barman, 'it's the tail-end of Europe and the asshole of the world.'

The barman just nodded and said, 'And you're just passing through yourself sir.'

Corkmen have a reputation of answering a question by asking another one. When this accusation was made against a Corkman, he replied 'Who told you that?'

It is said that a sociologist attempted to put a question to a Corkman that could be answered only 'yes' or 'no'. He stood in front of Cork's GPO and asked a passerby, 'Is that the post office?'

'Would it be a stamp you're wanting?' said the Corkman.

***

A Corkwoman went to the doctor and after he examined her he said, 'You've got acute paranoia.'

She retorted indignantly, 'I've come here to be examined, not to be admired.'

***

A Corkman's dog died so he went to the Bishop of Cork and asked if the dog could be buried in a Catholic graveyard.

'That's out of the question,' said the Bishop, 'it's forbidden by Canon Law.'

'That's a pity,' said the Corkman, 'I was prepared to donate a hundred thousand pounds towards the cost of the ceremony.'

'Hold on a minute,' said the Bishop, 'you didn't tell me the dog was a Catholic.'

THE CORK OPERA HOUSE

The Cork Opera Houses, both old and new, are a legendary source of humour and wit. There was a great tradition of audience participation there and at times it appears that many of the patrons went along with the express purpose of taking part in the show with contributions of devastating comment and wit. Here are some stories told about the Cork Opera House.

On one occasion a rather obscure Italian tenor was giving a concert in the Opera House. He was amazed that one aria he sang was given five encores. At the request for the sixth encore, he stepped forward and said, 'Never in my life before have I had such an enthusiastic reception anywhere. How many times must I perform this aria for you?'

Then a voice from the gods shouted out, 'You'll have to keep singing it until you get it right.'

On one occasion there was a performance of John B. Keane's famous drama *The Field* in the Opera House. In that play, the climax is reached when the field in question is up for auction. The tension was relieved when the audience enthusiastically joined in the bidding and the field was eventually sold by a very narrow margin to a member of the cast on stage.

Then there was the time that a British Dramatic Company were doing a week at the Opera House – a seasonal filler with a cast of fading television stars. The Opera House was only about a third full and the first act was diabolical. It consisted of a dialogue between a husband and wife in the living-room of a remote cottage. At the beginning of the second act there was a sharp knock on the door.

'I wonder who that could be?' asked the wife. A voice rang out from the back 'For God's sake, let them in whoever they are.'

In another production in the Opera House the hero and heroine appeared on stage and he whispered to her, 'Are we alone?' Before she got a chance to reply, a voice from the audience rang out 'no you're not, but tomorrow night you will be.'

Once there was a performance of the opera *Faust* in the Opera House and the entrance to hell was a trapdoor set in the middle of the stage. One evening, the part of the devil was being played by a very stout gentleman with a deep bass voice. As he attempted to descend into hell, he got stuck in the trapdoor and despite the best efforts of the cast to push him down, he remained wedged. The voice from the audience was not long in coming. 'Jaysus lads, great news. Hell is full.'

A massive religious revival meeting was once held in Cork and so many delegates were expected that the Opera House was chosen as a venue. One lady from the North of Ireland came on stage to tell of her religious experiences.

'Last night,' she said loudly, 'I was in the arms of Satan, but tonight I am in the arms of Jesus.'

An irreverent Cork evangelist shouted from the back, 'How are you fixed for tomorrow night?'

In the foyer of the Opera House after the premiere of one of his plays, a lady stopped John B. Keane and berated him publicly.

'Stand there,' she said, "till I give you a piece of my mind.'

'My dear woman,' said John B., 'your mind is so small that if you give me a bit of it you wouldn't have any left for yourself.'

$During$ a very boring performance of *The Diary of Ann Frank* when the Nazi soldiers broke into the house, a voice from the Opera House gods shouted 'She's under the stairs.'

A Dubliner, a Kerryman and a Corkman were about to be shot, so each is granted a last request.

'I'd like to have a last glass of whiskey,' said the Dubliner.

'I'd like to sing a sean-nós song,' said the Kerryman.

'I,' said the Corkman, 'would like to be shot before the Kerryman begins to sing.'

***

At the Cork railway station an American tourist asked a man in the bar if he had time for another drink before the train left.

'It all depends,' said the man, 'whether you're buying one for me or not, because I'm driving the train.'

***

A rather prim and proper Cork lady was a bit concerned about the number of gentlemen callers her maid was entertaining from time to time.

'Mary,' she said to her one evening, 'how do you feel about all those gentlemen who call on you?'

'Well,' said Mary, 'if I likes 'em I lets 'em and if I loves 'em I helps 'em.'

***

The famous Shandon Steeple has four faces with a clock on each face. Traditionally no two of these clocks tell the same time. An American tourist was intrigued by this, so he asked a Northsider to explain over a shared pint of the local brew.

'It's like this,' said the Northsider, 'sure if they all showed the same time, we'd need only one clock.'

***

The city of Cork can lay claim to be the only place on earth where a ship and a train collided. The incident took place on the bridge in front of City Hall which for many years had a railway track running along its length. A ship broke loose from its moorings in the Lee just as a train was passing by at high tide, and the two collided. Beat that!

***

A health conscious yuppie asked a stall holder in the covered market if there were any vitamins in her potatoes.

'Maybe there are a few,' she told him, 'but they'll die if you give it a good boiling.'

***

A six year old Cork boy went to his mother and said, 'Where did I come from?'

'Under the cabbage plant, son,' said his mother.

'And where did you and dad come from?'

'The stork brought us son.'

'And how about my four grandparents?'

'They came from under the gooseberry bush son.'

At this the little fellow fell silent, so his mother asked him what was wrong.

'I'm depressed,' he told her, 'for three generations there has been no sexual activity in my family.'

***

Have you heard that the Bishop of Cork has just sent a letter to all couples in the county who are faithful to each other?

Do you know what it said?

No? Didn't you get one then?

***

Jeremiah was staying in a dingy hotel. He complained to the manager that one of the walls of his room was so thin, he could almost see through it.

'That's your window, sir,' said the manager.

Con had great success betting on the horses, so his friend Jeremiah asked him what the secret was.

'Before every race,' said Con, 'I go to the Franciscan Church in Liberty Street, light six candles and pray for a bit and then place my bet. It's never known to fail yet.'

So Jeremiah went down to the Franciscan church on Liberty Street, lit six candles and prayed for a bit and headed for the bookies shop. He put everything he had on a horse called The Banks at a hundred to one and if the horse hadn't put a spurt on in the straight he wouldn't have finished first even in the next race.

That evening Jeremiah complained to his friend that things hadn't worked out.

'Did you go to the Franciscan church in Liberty Street like I told you?'

'I did.'

'And did you light six candles like I told you and pray a bit?'

'I did.'

'Tell me was it the big candles or the little candles you lit?'

'The small ones.'

'Ah you fool, that's where you went wrong. The small ones are for the dogs.'

***

CORK'S MRS MALAPROP

The character of Mrs Malprop first appeared in 1775 from the pen of Richard Brinsley Sheridan, the Irish dramatist, in a play called *The Rivals*. A malapropism has come to mean the replacing of one word or phrase with another of like sound but radically different meaning which conjures up a totally different image from the one intended. The best malapropisms are those where the new unintended meaning is often a more appropriate description of the situation than the original.

Cork, I have found, is teeming with latter-day Mrs Malaprops, and Mr Malaprops too. These creative geniuses show us the extraordinary richness of language, revealing hidden connections between words and concepts in a way that the great Fraud would have envied. Here are a few of the best malapropisms I have come across in Cork – all of them genuine.

If the ambulance had arrived in time they could have survived and resufficated him.

In hospital he got the RIP treatment.

The octopus wrapped his testicles around her.

My daughter took up cookery and was awarded the condom bleu.

She bought a pelvis on which to hang her curtains.

He is a defective in the police farce.

For winter I'm going to buy some terminal underwear.

Jesus was betrayed by Judas the Carrycot.

And Mary was exposed to a man named Joseph.

The Pope is inflammable.

Solomon had 500 wives and 700 cucumbers.

She spent a lot of time in the toilet – she had dire rear.

He had ulsters in his stomach.

I don't agree with unmarried people corabbiting together.

There he was standing starch naked on the beach.

She's in the Bone Sick Cure Hospital.

He's taking part in the Government's Job Cremation Scheme.

She hasn't been to the toilet for a week. She has consternation.

They're in the first careless rupture of love.

The law is too laxative on criminals.

I like to drink decapitated coffee.

The lifeguard gave her artificial insemination.

They went to Cuba and met Fidel Castrato.

I met the lad who's her daughter's fiasco.

The French national anthem – you know, the Mayonnaise.

The French are always having general erections.

I take everything she said with a dose of salts.

The patron saint of animals is Francis of Onassis.

Surely good Mrs Murphy will follow me all the days of my life and I will dwell in the house of the Lord forever.

She had all those needles stuck in her – acapulco.

She had the mentalpause and had her aviaries removed.

She had a epiduracell and a cistercian section.

The Japanese warrior committed cash and carry.

Her son is a lecherer in sociology.

She cannot take sugar. She's a diabolic.

They gave her a standing ovulation.

She gave away all her blankets and bought bidets instead.

A Corkwoman goes into hospital to have her tenth baby and she is attended by the same doctor who has delivered the other nine.

'That's the tenth child you've had by this man,' he says to her after the delivery, 'why don't you marry him?'

'No, doctor, I couldn't do that,' she says.

'You owe it to the kids and to yourself,' he says.

'No, I couldn't do that under any circumstances, doctor.'

'And why not?' he asked her.

'Well, you see doctor,' she told him, 'I never really liked him.'

***

A man bought a pair of trousers at Cork's famous open air market on the Coal Quay but when he took them home and tried them on he was annoyed to find that half of one of the legs was missing. When he took them back to complain, the woman in charge of the stall said before he could open his mouth, 'I knew you'd be back sir, you forgot to take the crutch that was with them trousers.'

***

A Cork restaurant owner received a phone booking for a dinner reservation from a traffic warden and two friends.

He decided it was a hoax call because no traffic warden has that many friends.

***

'How heavy was the latest child your wife had?' Con asked Jeremiah.

'Two pounds, three ounces,' replied Jeremiah.

'Hell man,' said Con, 'you hardly got your bait back.'

***

A humble Cork labourer was selected for the Irish rugby team and eventually made the team that travelled to play test matches in Australia and New Zealand. On his return, he was asked how he liked mixing with all the upper class, highly educated players on the team.

'It was pretty difficult at times,' he told them, 'they were always using big words like "galvanise" and "marmalade".'

***

Con and his wife Bernadette were coming home together from a mission where a trendy young missioner had been preaching on the sixth commandment.

'Tell me Con, did you understand all that?'

'Of course I did, woman,' said Con.

'Well, tell me, do we have any sexual relations?'

'Of course we do,' said Con.

'Well how is it we never hear from them, not even a card at Christmas?'

***

A young Cork lad was being interviewed for a job.

'Where were your father and mother from?' asked the interviewer.

'I never had a father and mother sir,' he replied, 'someone interfered with my aunt.'

***

When the Second World War was declared in 1939 a Parish Priest in a West Cork village stood up to preach one Sunday.

'I never thought,' he told his flock, 'that in my lifetime we would again see global conflict. But let me tell you that it is not Adolph Hitler that is responsible, nor the invasion of Poland – it is the goings on down the Clonakilty Road.'

A famous Cork story relates how a rather upper-class Corkman (from the Rochestown Road, no doubt) came out of the lounge of a city pub to use the telephone.

'Is that you, Raymond?' he phoned for all to hear, 'spot of bad news actually. I cannot take part in the hunt tomorrow. The mare has strained a fetlock.'

Sitting in the bar listening to all this was a little Northsider, with a peaked cap, sipping his pint. After a few minutes, he went over to the phone, dialled and said, 'Is dat you Mossy? I can't make it to the hunt tomorrow because de ferret have de flu.'

***

Jeremiah went into a new posh Cork restaurant and ordered bacon and cabbage. He was served with the most miserly portion he could imagine.

'Is there anything the matter sir?' asked the waiter, as he watched Jeremiah looking at his portion.

'I usually *leave* more than that,' said Jeremiah.

QUIZ TIME

Over the years I have collected a great many answers to the questions asked in quizzes in Cork – Quicksilver, pub quizzes and table quizzes. Many of these probably stem from panic in the contestants or perhaps stage fright, but there is an old Cork principle that if you don't know the right answer, you might as well give the audience a laugh for their money. In fact, it probably takes more wit and ingenuity to compose a funny wrong answer than to give a boringly correct one. Here were a few of the most ingenious answers I have heard.

What is a male bee called?
A wasp.

What are your parent's names?
Mammy and Daddy.

Name two days of the week beginning with the letter 'T'.
Today and tomorrow.

Who was the Ayatollah?
He was the fellow who started up the céilí band.

What is an oscillator?
A Connemara man who eats donkeys.

What is a Biafran?
A fellow who goes to mass twice on Sundays.

What was Gandhi's first name?
Would it be Goosey Goosey?

What goes green, amber, red, green, amber, red?
A packet of fruit gums.

What do the letters AIB stand for?
Artificial Insemination by a Bull.

Why is a giraffe's neck so long?
Because his head is so far away from his body.

To which family does the whale belong?
I don't know. Nobody near me has one anyway.

Where is the lumbar region in anatomy?
Is it near the north of Canada?

What is backgammon?
It's a sort of rasher.

How many degrees in a circle?
How big a circle are you talking about?

How do you spell Tipperary?
Do you mean the town now or the county?

What was general amnesty?
He was the Supreme Commander of the Allied Forces during the Second World War.

***

Cork graffiti
Keep death off the roads –
Drive on the footpath.

***

A old Cork Christian Brother was asked if he ever used audio-visual aids.

He replied: 'Do you see this stick, and do you hear what I'm saying?'

Cork graffiti

Keep Cork clean –
dump your litter in Kerry.

***

A venerable Cork doctor had a morbid fear of dogs so his first question on being called out to see a patient was always 'any dogs?' In typical Cork fashion, he eventually became known as 'any dogs'. There is a story of him being called to see a sick baby and on being told there was a dog in the house went into a house across the road and had the mother hold her baby out the bedroom window across the street, whereupon he made an instant diagnosis of the child's condition!

***

They say you can always tell a Corkman – but you can't tell him much.

***

They say that a true Corkman is a fellow who would trample over the bodies of twelve naked women to reach a pint of porter.

The Most Reverend Doctor Cornelius Lucey, affectionately known as 'Connie', was for many years the Bishop of Cork. He was a strict man, always ready to carry out the regulations of the Church to the letter. During one Lent, a discussion arose among the laity if it was allowable to take biscuits with a mid-morning cup of tea or coffee or if this broke the fast. Dr Lucey gave as his infallible opinion that the faithful were allowed one and only one biscuit with a cup of tea or coffee. An enterprising Cork firm of confectioners however, immediately put on the market biscuits nearly twelve inches in diameter which became known far and wide as 'Connie Dodgers'.

***

When tenders were being sought for Cork's new tunnel under the river Lee, two out of work labourers arrived up in the City Manager's office and offered to do the job for £500.

'But how can you do the job for that price?' asked the City Manager.

'Easy,' said Con, 'I'll start with my shovel on the south side, while my colleague Jeremiah here will start digging on the north side of the river with his shovel and that will cut the work time in half.'

'But what happens,' said the City Manager, 'if you miscalculate and fail to meet in the middle?'

'In that case,' said Con, 'you get two tunnels for the price of one.'

A Cork businessman was worried that a colleague of his wasn't doing too well. He told his wife that he was at the man's house a few nights previously and saw his two daughters sitting together playing on the one piano.

***

In Cork, change is inevitable – except from vending machines.

***

There was a landlady in Cork who took in students. The digs were terrific but she was the most inquisitive woman in the world, and many students left on this account.

'Where were you last night?' she would ask. 'Who were you with and how many drinks did you have?' and so on until she nearly drove them around the bend.

One day she had a chimney sweep in cleaning the chimney for the winter fires and she was driving the poor man out of his mind with questions. 'How do you know now that that's the right brush to use? How do you know it won't get stuck up there?' And so on. Finally she asked him, 'How long have you been a chimney sweep?'

'About thirty years ma'am.'

'And how did you become a chimney sweep?'

He looked at her and said, 'I took a correspondence course.'

A West Cork lad had emigrated to London and wandered into a pub.

'Give us a pint of Guinness there,' he said to the bar man.

'Look Paddy,' said the barman, 'this is a gay pub, you might be better off elsewhere.'

'Yerra, 'tis all the wan to me what sort of pub it is, give me that pint.' So the barman did.

Later on that evening a fellow came up to the Cork lad and asked him if he would like a room for the night, so off they went together. The next night, the barman was a bit worried, so when the Cork lad came in again, he asked him how he had got on.

'Great altogether,' said the lad, 'lashings of drink and food, and my own room for the night.'

'And did anything peculiar happen?' asked the barman.

'Well come to think of it,' said the lad, 'at about two o'clock in the morning, your man appeared in my bedroom, dressed in nothing but a pair of rubber underpants and carrying a whip. He said "I've been a naughty boy, I've been late for school. You'll have to spank me".'

'And what happened then?'

'By God I'll tell you wan thing, he'll never be late for school again.'

***

It has been said that the ideal wife for a Corkman is a rich dumb blonde nymphomaniac who owns a pub near a golf course.

***

Two little Cork brothers were always late for school, one of them always fifteen minutes later than the other. So one day the teacher decided to ask them why.

'I had to eat a boiled egg for my breakfast, sir,' said the first young lad.

'And why were you late?' he asked the second lad.

'I had to eat a boiled egg for my breakfast too, sir.'

'But why were you fifteen minutes later than your brother?'

'Had I a spoon, had I?'

***

Jeremiah's wife died but as they were bringing her coffin down the narrow stairs of their house, it hit against the banisters and the 'dead' woman sat right up, right as rain and demanded her dinner. She lived for twenty more years. Then this time she really did die, and as they once again brought the coffin down the narrow stairs Jeremiah went 'steady lads, careful now, don't bang it against anything'.

Con was taking part in a big quiz show with all his friends present.

'Now for £500,' said the quizmaster, 'what is it a man does standing up that a woman does sitting down?'

'Shakes hands,' said Con.

'Correct,' said the quizmaster. 'Now for £5,000, what is it goes in dry, comes out wet, and gives pleasure to two people?'

'A tea bag,' said Con.

'Correct,' said the quizmaster. 'Now for the £10,000 question, you go into the soundproof booth and you can take one person in with you to help you.'

'I'll take the Parish Priest,' said Con.

'It's no use taking me,' said the Parish Priest, 'I got the first two answers wrong.'

***

A fanatical Irish speaking Corkman went into a restaurant and ordered a bowl of soup. To his disgust, there was a fly in it, so he called the waiter and pointed to it.

'O, an cuiléog,' said the waiter.

'It's not "an cuiléog", it's "an chuiléog",' said the gaelgóir, 'it's feminine.'

'Haven't you great eyesight?' said the waiter.

***

A woman emigrated from Cork to New Zealand in her twenties and returned for a holiday in Cork. By this time she had more than a touch of a Kiwi accent.

On her first day home, she went into a shop to buy a packet of mints so she put a ten pound note on the counter. For her change she got about two pounds.

'Hang on,' she said to the man in the shop, 'I gave you ten pounds.'

'Sorry ma'am,' said the man, 'I thought you were a tourist.'

***

Cork's most famous son, Paddy Murphy, went to Hollywood, changed his name to Bruno Silverstein and became a major film star, picking up several Oscars in the process. After twenty years he felt a burning desire to return to Cork, so he came back, stood at the railway station with his suitcase hoping to see some old friends.

Right enough one of them sauntered up to him and said, 'Howya Paddy. Are you thinking of leaving town?'

A local came up to a man in a bar in Cork and said, 'You're a stranger here aren't you?'

'Yes,' said the man, a bit taken aback, 'how did you know?'

'You took your hand off the glass,' said the Corkman.

***

The world's strongest man was performing his act in Cork. He took a lemon and with his huge hands squeezed nearly a pint of juice out of it.

'I now offer a hundred pounds,' he announced, 'to anybody who can squeeze another drop of juice from that lemon.'

There was a huge laugh as a tiny little man with a bowler hat in the audience rose from his seat and made his way to the stage. The laughter turned to gasps of astonishment as he proceeded to squeeze over half a cup of lemon juice from what the strong man had left behind him.

As the MC handed over the hundred pounds he asked the man what he did for a living.

The man replied with a smile, 'I'm an income tax inspector.'

***

A Corkman and his wife were painting their house. She was up on the ladder painting away while he was directing operations from the ground.

'Have you got a firm grip on that brush?' he asked her.

'I have,' she replied.

'Well hold on tight,' he told her, 'because I'm taking the ladder away.'

***

Here's a practical joke sometimes played in Cork. You drive down Patrick Street until you meet an unsuspecting tourist. You say to him, 'Excuse me, do you know the way to Montenotte?'

When he says, 'I'm terribly sorry, I don't', you say, 'Well, you drive across Patrick's Bridge, along McCurtain Street, up the Hill to St Luke's, turn right, and there you are. Right?' And then you drive off.

A Cork businessman who had left school at the age of fourteen was giving a lecture to the Chamber of Commerce on how he had made his millions. His audience, full of B. Comms, accountants and business school graduates, could not understand his business methods, 'It's quite simple, gentlemen,' he told them. 'I'm a simple man. I buy an object for one pound and sell it for two pounds. I'm not greedy. I'm quite happy with my one percent profit!'

***

Con was thinking of getting a new set of false teeth so he asked his friend Jeremiah if he would recommend the dentist from whom he got his false teeth.

'Well,' said Jeremiah, 'I was passing a building site the other day and a large brick fell from over a hundred feet. I tried to avoid it but it hit me right in the wedding tackle.'

'That's sad,' said Con, 'but what has that to do with my query?'

'Well,' said Jeremiah, 'that's the first time in six weeks I forgot about the pain those false teeth were causing me.'

***

A drunk strolled into a Cork fish and chip shop one night and said, 'Could I have *Gone with the Wind* please?'

'I'm sorry,' said the assistant, 'this is a fish and chip shop, not a video rental outlet.'

A few minutes later he was back – 'Would you have *The Quiet Man*?'

'Look,' said the assistant, a bit annoyed, 'this is a fish and chip shop and we don't have any videos.'

A few minutes later he was back once again.

'Would you have a fish?'

'That's better,' said the assistant.

'Called Wanda?' said the drunk.

HUMOROUS QUOTATIONS

Des MacHale

Do you know who said:

'I always arrive late at the office, but make up for it by leaving early.'

'I wish dear Karl could have spent some time acquiring capital instead of merely writing about it.'

'When I came back to Dublin I was courtmartialled in my absence and sentenced to death in my absence, so I said they could shoot me in my absence.'

'Insanity is hereditary; you can get it from your children.'

'He who throws mud loses ground.'

THE BOOK OF IRISH BULL

Des MacHale

Notices:

To touch these wires means instant death – anyone who does so will be prosecuted.

No fishing allowed on this land.

These lands are poisoned for the protection of game.

Definition of a coffin:
'A coffin is a house a man lives in after he is dead.'

***

The finest sight in Dublin is the smell of the Liffey.

***

'Sterility is hereditary – if your parents and grand-parents didn't have any children, the chances are that you won't have any either.'

***

A verbal argument is not worth the paper it is written on.

THE BOOK OF
KERRYMAN JOKES

Des MacHale

There is only one explanation for the spate of Kerryman jokes that has engulfed Ireland like a tidal wave for the last fifteen years or so – jealousy. After all, Kerry has won the all-Ireland football title more often than any other county; it has the beautiful Lakes of Killarney, held by so many to have the most magificent scenery in the world; and it has the Rose of Tralee competition, featuring the loveliest and most charming girls one can imagine. In addition, recent historical and religious research by John B. Keane seems to suggest that even the Holy Ghost was a Kerryman.

THE BUMPER BOOK OF
KERRYMAN JOKES

Des MacHale

How do you recognise a Kerryman in a shoeshop?

How does a Kerryman forge 10p pieces?

How do you recognise a Kerry bath?

Have you heard about the Kerry video recorder?

How do you sink a Kerry submarine?